STARTING SCHOOL

Caryn Jenner & Arthur Robins

W
FRANKLIN WATTS

Notes for parents and carers

Starting a new school can be daunting.
This book helps to prepare your child – and you!

Use this book to give your child an idea of what to expect at school. Find out what he or she is looking forward to most. If your child is worried, point out how the children in this book resolve difficulties. This will help boost their confidence. Be enthusiastic about school and your child will be, too!

A few more ideas before the big day...

★ Visit the school beforehand. Try and meet the teacher and other children in the class.

★ Have some practice runs to school in the weeks leading up to the first day.

★ Help your child to be more independent with skills such as using the toilet and getting dressed.

This edition published in 2012 by
Franklin Watts
338 Euston Road
London NW1 3BH

Franklin Watts Australia
Level 17/207 Kent Street
Sydney NSW 2000

With thanks to Southfield Primary School and Shayne Johnson.

A CIP catalogue record for this book is available from the British Library.

ISBN: 978 1 4451 0095 1

Printed in China

Franklin Watts is a division of Hachette Children's Books, an Hachette UK company.
www.hachette.co.uk

To Lia, my very curious daughter – C.J.

Contents

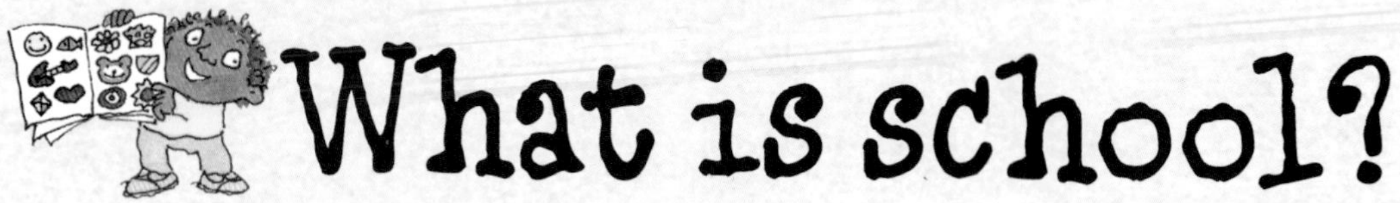

What is school?

Lucky you!

You're starting school soon.

School is a place to learn, try new things,

and have fun!

Other children will be starting school too, and you'll make lots of new friends.

Getting ready

In the mornings, everyone must get to school on time. Sometimes it's a rush to get ready!

I get my school clothes ready the night before. In the morning, I get dressed **quick as a flash!**

At our school we wear uniforms. Our school badge is on the sweatshirt.

A good breakfast gives me lots of energy for school.
I'm having two bowls!
I put everything I need in my school bag ready to bring with me.
I take tiny teddy in my pocket. He is very well-behaved!

Arriving at school

All the children must arrive by the time school starts.

We walk to school. Sometimes we have to run so we aren't late!

My friends and I take the bus to school.

My dad drives me to school. He drops me off at the school entrance where my teacher meets us.

We queue up
to go into school
with our teacher.
Oops!
The bell's gone.
I'm late!

Morning routine

The children know what to do when they go into school every morning. Soon, you'll learn your morning routine, too.

First, I hang my coat on my peg. The peg has my name and a picture on it.

As soon as I go into my classroom, I sit quietly in my special place on the carpet.

Every morning, our teacher takes the register.
We have to be quiet so we can listen for our names.
When she calls my name, I say, "Good morning, Miss." Then she marks a tick in her register book.
Good morning, Miss!

In the classroom

The classroom is full of interesting things.
What do you think you'll find in your classroom?

Everyone in my class has a tray where we keep our things.

There's paper and lots of pens and pencils for writing and drawing.

The reading corner has lots of books. Yesterday, our teacher read this one. **It was so funny!**

I **love** *the pictures in this book.*

at
bat
cat
hat
We're playing a rhyming game at the whiteboard.
pat
rat
In the dressing-up corner, we play pretend games.
May I help you, your highness?
I'd like a tin of your best soup, please!
We wear aprons in the messy area where we do painting and sticking.
I'm painting my mum!

People at school

Everyone at school is really nice.
It's their job to help children like you.

The headteacher is in charge of the whole school.
This is my teacher. She is in charge of my class.

The caretaker looks
after the school building.

The first-aider makes
the children feel better.

Hi, Dad!
Hi, Mum!
Hi,
doughnut!

Lots of mums and dads
help out at school, too.

Around the school

School can seem like a very big place.
But after a while you'll learn your way around.

The people in the office help to organise the school. Ask them if you have any questions.

If you get lost, there's always someone around to help.

A
E
B
Excuse me, I can't find my class!

The school library has all sorts of books.
In the ICT room, we learn to use computers. It's like a grown-up office!
At my school, we use the hall for lots of different things. In the mornings, we have assembly here...
...at lunchtime, we eat here...
... and in the afternoons, we use it for PE lessons. PE means exercise and games.

School toilets

If you need the toilet at school, just raise your hand and ask your teacher. Don't try to hold it in!

The toilets are just the right size for children.
I always wash my hands after.
I don't even need to stand on my toes to reach the sink.

School rules

Everyone at school has to follow rules.
These rules make school a safe and happy place.

Raise your hand and wait for your turn to speak.

Do you want a go?

Take turns and share.

It's your school, so keep it tidy.

LITTER

Shhhh!
Walk quietly
in the corridors.

Be kind, helpful
and polite.

Listen carefully so
you know what to do.

Follow directions.

That means do what your teacher says!

What we learn

You'll be learning lots of new things at school. Some things might be easy-peasy, but others will be a bit harder. Just try your best.

We're learning about letters and the sounds they make.

1 2 3 4 5 6 7 8 9 10
I'm learning my numbers.
I'm learning about plants. This plant started as a tiny seed.
eye
nose
ear
mouth
Can you guess what I'm learning about?

Playtime

There's time to run around and play at school, too.

Yippee!
It's playtime!
Our class plays in this playground, but the big children play over there.
If I don't know who to play with, I ask somebody if I can join their game.

In the playground, our rules are to play safely ...
... and be kind to each other!
We share the toys so that everyone has a turn.
Can I have a go next?
When it's raining, we have indoor playtime.
There are books and games to keep us busy.

Lunchtime

Learning is hungry work, so eat a good lunch! Some children bring a packed lunch, and others have school dinners.

If I don't know where to sit, I just find an empty seat. Hi, I'm Jack.

I'm Jill. I've got a cheese sandwich. What about you?

We all have to stay in our seats at lunchtime.

I ask if I need some help to cut my food.

If we're getting school dinners, we wait in the queue.
I've got pasta - my favourite!
I used to be a fussy eater, but now I try lots of different foods.
Remember to say please and thank you.
I'm so hungry!

Special days

Some days at school are extra special and extra fun!

It's Book Day. I'm dressed up as my favourite book character – the Big Bad Wolf.

Nee-naw, nee-naw! The Fire Brigade is visiting our school to talk about fire safety.

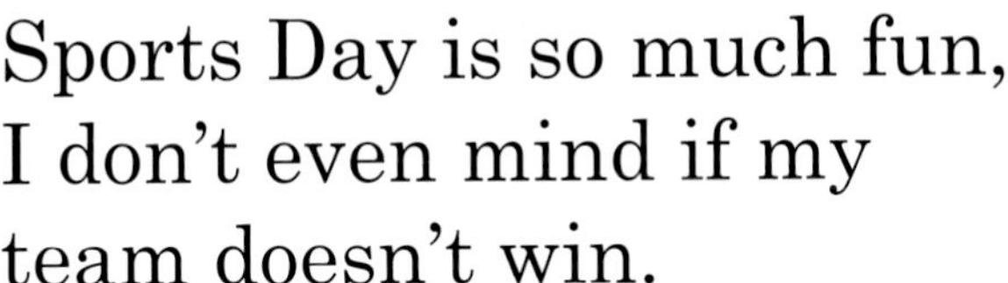

Sports Day is so much fun, I don't even mind if my team doesn't win.

Oops!

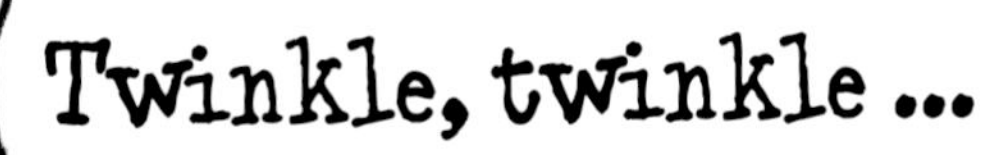
Twinkle, twinkle ...

Today, our class is doing an assembly for the whole school! I hope I remember the song.

We're on a school trip today. Can you guess where we are?

Favourite things

This is what some children say about school. Soon this will be you. Have fun!

We do lots of fun things at my school.

I'm learning to read. That's my favourite thing!

I love it when I learn to do something new. It's a brilliant feeling!

I like school because I'm really curious. School is a good place to learn about things.
I like playing with my friends.
I like getting stickers. This one is for trying hard, and this one is for good behaviour.
I love my teacher!
My mum says I like filling my brain with facts. She's right!

We love school!